Looking at Rocks

by Elizabeth Moore

W9-DHR-812

SKOKIE PUBLIC LIBRARY

3 1232 00701 2083

JUL   2013

Consultant:
Adria F. Klein, PhD
California State University, San Bernardino

CAPSTONE PRESS
a capstone imprint

Wonder Readers are published by Capstone Press,
1710 Roe Crest Drive, North Mankato, Minnesota 56003.
www.capstonepub.com

Copyright © 2013 by Capstone Press, a Capstone imprint. All rights reserved.
No part of this publication may be reproduced in whole or in part, or stored in a retrieval system, or
transmitted in any form or by any means, electronic, mechanical, photocopying, recording, or otherwise,
without written permission of the publisher. For information regarding permission, *write* to Capstone Press,
1710 Roe Crest Drive, North Mankato, Minnesota 56003.

Library of Congress Cataloging-in-Publication Data
Moore, Elizabeth.
  Looking at rocks / Elizabeth Moore.—1st ed.
    p. cm.—(Wonder readers)
Includes index.
ISBN 978-1-4765-0037-9 (library binding)
ISBN 978-1-4296-7809-4 (paperback)
ISBN 978-1-4765-0850-4 (eBook pdf)
1. Rocks—Juvenile literature. I. Title. II. Series.
  QE432.2.M65 2013
  552—dc23   2011023097

Summary: Describes the study of rocks and how people use them.

Editorial Credits
Maryellen Gregoire, project director; Mary Lindeen, consulting editor; Gene Bentdahl, designer;
Sarah Schuette, editor; Wanda Winch, media researcher; Eric Manske, production specialist

Photo Credits
Capstone Studio: Karon Dubke, 1, 4, 13, 15, 18, TJ Thoraldson Digital Photography, 17; Shutterstock:
aceshot1, 16, Andry N Bannov, 14, Ariel Bravy, 8, Chun-Tso Lin, 11, Darren J. Bradley, 10, Djusha, 6, Dmit
Vinogradov, 7, dymon, 5, Orla, cover, Rich Koele, 12, thoron, 9

Word Count: **200**   Guided Reading Level: **H**   Early Intervention Level: **1**

Printed in China.
092012   006934LEOS13

Table of Contents

Note to Parents and Teachers

The Wonder Readers Next Steps: Science series supports national science standards. These titles use text structures that support early readers, specifically with a close photo/text match and glossary. Each book is perfectly leveled to support the reader at the right reading level, and the topics are of high interest. Early readers will gain success when they are presented with a book that is of interest to them and is written at the appropriate level.

Rocks Everywhere

Rocks are everywhere.
You can see rocks in the park.
Let's look at rocks up close.

Rocks are in rivers and lakes.

Rock covers our Earth.

Mountains are made of rocks.

Some beaches have small rocks.
Other beaches have sand.
Sand is rock too.

The Story of Earth

Rocks tell us the story of Earth.
They show where rock was worn
down by water.

The lines of color in the rock show how Earth changed over time.

Rain, wind, and ice made
this rock **arch**.

Cold and hot weather made
these rock joints.

Some rocks have traces
of animals and plants in them.
These traces are called **fossils**.

We can find out when these plants and animals lived by looking at their fossils.

Using Rocks

People use rocks. They build houses out of rocks. Crushed rocks are used to build roads, bridges, airports, and parking lots.

People use rocks to make **statues** and decorate buildings.

Rocks can also be used for making
jewelry. All through history,
kings and queens have used rocks
in their jewelry.

Rocks are even used at school. Graphite is a rock. It is the part of a pencil that makes a mark.

Rocks are interesting.

Take the time to look at rocks!

Now Try This!

Flip to a page in this book. Write down the first sentence on the page. Do this three times with three different sentences. Now look at the table of contents. The information about rocks presented in this book is divided into three sections: Rocks Everywhere (where rocks can be found), The Story of Earth (how rocks tell us about the planet), and Using Rocks (what people do with rocks). Read the sentences you've written aloud. After you read each sentence, write which section of the book you think that sentence came from. How did you know which section to guess?

Glossary

rch	a curved, open formation in rock
ossil	the remains or traces of an animal or a plant, preserved as rock
tatue	a model of a person or an animal made from metal, stone, or wood

Internet Sites

FactHound offers a safe, fun way to find Internet sites related to this book. All of the sites on FactHound have been researched by our staff.

Here's all you do:

Visit *www.facthound.com*

Type in this code: 9781476500379

Check out projects, games and lots more at
www.capstonekids.com

Index